Sing it in the morning

Selected by
Geoffrey Clifton, M.A., A.R.M.C.M.

Nelson

Thomas Nelson and Sons Ltd
36 Park Street London W1Y 4DE
PO Box 18123 Nairobi Kenya

Thomas Nelson (Australia) Ltd
19–39 Jeffcott Street West Melbourne
Victoria 3003

Thomas Nelson and Sons (Canada) Ltd
81 Curlew Drive Don Mills Ontario

Thomas Nelson (Nigeria) Ltd
PO Box 336 Apapa Lagos

First published 1975
Second impression 1975

First published 1974

Acknowledgements—The copyright acknowledgements are printed beneath each item. Every effort has been made to trace copyright owners. The publishers apologise for any omissions, which will be rectified in subsequent reprints.

Cover design: Permission to use music and words of *If I Had a Hammer* granted by TRO Essex Music Ltd.

0 17 4280084

Printed in Spain
By Editorial Eléxpuru Hnos., S. A. - Bilbao
Depósito legal - BI - 1.654 - 1975

Contents

Friendship

1 Think, Think on These Things

1
Think, think on these things:
Being a friend,
Giving a smile,
Or helping to make
Someone else's day
  worthwhile;
Think, think on these things.

2
Think, think on these things:
Unhappy and lost,
Friendless or old,
Or what it is like
To be hungry, to be cold;
Think, think on these things.

3
Think, think on these things:
Forgiving an ill,
Lending a hand,
Or trying to make
Other people understand;
Think, think on these things.

Peggy Blakeley

Look Out for Loneliness

2

1

Look out for loneliness
If it should come your way,
Look out for loneliness,
Watch for it every day.
Look at home, look in school,
When you're walking in the
  street,
In the park and at the bus
  stop,
In the faces that you meet.
  Look out, look out, look out
  For loneliness.

2

Look out for strangers
Every once in a while,
Look out for strangers
Who need a friendly smile.
Give some love,
Give some warmth,
Give a hand in welcome too;
Bear in mind that one day
  soon
That stranger may quite well
  be you.
  Look out, look out, look out
  For loneliness.

Peggy Blakeley

3 There's A Road

1
There's a road which leads from Jerusalem,
It's the way down to Jericho,
It's Compassion road, steep and tiring road,
Which has danger from thieving foe.
And here on this road is one man
Beaten up and left as half dead,
Like many in this world around us
Oppressed, in despair or unfed.
Hear him cry out
As he lies on Compassion road.

2
Watch a priest and levite come down that road
Only giving the man small heed,
They are too caught up with religious thoughts
To give help to a man in need.
Samaritan, walk behind them!
You are not within the same class!
But you are the one who helps him—
You could not see need and just pass!
You heard the cry
As you walked on Compassion road.

3
The Compassion road goes right on through life,
It's a road with us still today,
Many hands are needed to give the help
To those stricken upon the way.
So now will you have compassion?
To the lonely, hungry, and worn.
To those without hope or salvation
To fearful and poor and forlorn?
Lord, give us grace
To give help on Compassion road.

M. G. Schneider

Feed Us Now

4

Feed us now, O Son of God,
As you fed them long ago.

1
The people came to hear you,
The poor, the lame, the blind.
They asked for food and shelter
And you fed them body and mind.

2
The ones who didn't listen,
The rich, the safe, the sure,
They didn't think they needed
The offering of a cure.

3
It's hard for us to listen.
Things haven't changed at all.
We've got the things we wanted.
We don't want to hear your call.

4
Yet millions still have hunger,
Disease, no homes and fear.
We offer them so little
And it costs them very dear.

5
So help us see the writing
Written clear upon the wall.
He who doesn't feed his neighbour
Will get no food at all.

Peter Allen

5 Pilgrim's Hymn

1
We ask that we live and we labour in peace, in peace.
Each man shall be our neighbour in peace, in peace.
Distrust and hatred will turn to love,
All the prisoners freed,
And our only war will be the one
Against all human need.

2
We work for the end of disunion in truth, in truth.
That all may be one in communion in truth, in truth.
We choose the road of peace and prayer
Countless pilgrims trod,
So that Hindu, Moslem, Christian, Jew
We all can worship one God.

3
We call to our friends and brothers, unite, unite!
That all may live for others, unite, unite!
And so the nations will be as one,
One the flag unfurled,
One law, one faith, one hope, one truth,
One people and one world.

Donald Swann

Shalom

Shalom, good friends,
Shalom, good friends,
Shalom, shalom!

Till we meet again,
Till we meet again,
Shalom, shalom!

Traditional

7 I Belong to a Family

1
I belong to a family,
the biggest on earth,
A thousand every day are
coming to birth.
Our name isn't Dallas or
Hasted or Jones,
It's the name every man
should be proud he owns:

It's the family of man,
keeps growing,
The family of man,
keeps sowing
The seeds of a new life
every day.

2
I've got a sister in
Melbourne, and brother in
Paree,
The whole wide world is dad
and mother to me.
Wherever you turn you will
find my kin,
Whatever the creed or the
colour of skin.
It's the family of man . . .

3
The miner in the Rhondda,
the coolie in Pekin,
Men across the world who
reap and plough and spin,
They've got a life and others
to share it,
Let's bridge the oceans and
declare it:
It's the family of man . . .

4
From the North Pole ice to
the snow at the other,
There isn't a man I wouldn't
call my brother;
But I haven't much time,
I've had my fill
Of the men of war who want
to kill.
It's the family of man . . .

5
Some people say the world
is a horrible place,
But it's just as good or bad
as the human race;
Dirt and misery or health
and joy,
Man can build or can
destroy;
It's the family of man . . .

Fred Dallas

Magic Penny

*Love is something if you
give it away,
Give it away, give it away,
Love is something if you
give it away,
You end up having more.*

1
It's just like a magic penny;
Hold it tight and you won't
have any;
Lend it, spend it, and you'll
have so many,
They'll roll all over the floor,
for:
Love is something . . .

2
So let's go dancing till the
break of day,
And if there's a piper,
we can pay.
For love is something if
you give it away,
You end up having more.
Love is something . . .

Malvina Reynolds

9 No Miracles Today

1
No miracles today,
no sign which makes us say
to one another,
"The Lord is here to stay,"
unless a man holds out his
hand towards his brother.

2
No miracles today,
no sign which makes us say
to one another,
"The Lord is here to stay,"
unless a man will fight for
justice for his brother.

3
No miracles today,
no sign which makes us say
to one another,
"The Lord is here to stay,"
unless a man lays down his
life to save his brother.

4
No miracles today,
no sign which makes us say
to one another,
"The Lord is here to stay,"
unless a man who once was
dead now calls us brother.

Michael Cockett

Black and White

1
The ink is black, the page is
white,
Together we learn to read
and write, to read and
write,
And now a child can
understand
This is the law of all the land;
all the land;
The ink is black,
the page is white,
Together we learn to read
and write, to read and
write.

2
The slate is black,
the chalk is white,
The words stand out so clear
and bright,
so clear and bright,
And now at last we plainly
see
The alphabet of liberty;
liberty;
The slate is black,
the chalk is white,
Together we learn to
read and write,
to read and write.

3
A child is black,
a child is white,
The whole world looks
upon the sight,
upon the sight,
For very well the whole
world knows
This is the way that freedom
grows,
freedom grows,
A child is black,
a child is white,
Together we learn
to read and write,
to read and write.

4
The world is black,
the world is white,
In turns by day
and then by night,
and then by night,
It turns so each and every one
Can take his station
in the sun,
in the sun,
The world is black,
the world is white,
Together we learn
to read and write,
to read and write.

David Arkin

11 If I Had a Hammer

1
If I had a hammer,
  I'd hammer in the morning,
I'd hammer in the evening,
  all over this land;
I'd hammer out danger,
  I'd hammer out a warning,
I'd hammer out love
  between all of my brothers,
All over this land.

2
If I had a bell,
  I'd ring it in the morning,
I'd ring it in the evening,
  all over this land;
I'd ring out danger,
  I'd ring out a warning,
I'd ring out love
  between all of my brothers,
All over this land.

3
If I had a song,
  I'd sing it in the morning,
I'd sing it in the evening,
  all over this land;
I'd sing out danger,
  I'd sing out a warning,
I'd sing out love
  between all of my brothers,
All over this land.

4
Well I've got a hammer,
  and I've got a bell,
And I've got a song to sing
  all over this land;
It's the hammer of justice,
  it's the bell of freedom,
It's the song about love
  between all of my brothers,
All over this land.

Pete Seeger and Lee Hays

Gentle Christ

1
The soldier's came at Pilate's call,
Led him into the common hall,
Took sharp thorns and made a crown
Dressed him in a scarlet gown.
Gentle Christ, wise and good,
We nailed him to a cross of wood.
The Son of God, he lived to save
In borrowed stable and borrowed grave.

2
They spat on him and mocked him then,
Lashed his back again and again,
Laid that cross upon his back,
Forced him up that narrow track.
Gentle Christ . . .

3
The soldiers hung him on the cross,
Played for his clothes at pitch and toss,
When each of them had won a share,
Sitting down they watched him there.
Gentle Christ . . .

4
We say as many would say today
We wouldn't have treated our Saviour that way,
But Gentle Christ wise and good,
We nailed him to a cross of wood.
Gentle Christ . . .

Mike Gwilliam
From 'A Man Dies'
by Ernest Marvin and Ewan Hooper

13 The Angel Rolled the Stone Away

The angel rolled the stone away,
The angel rolled the stone away,
'Twas on a bright and shiny morn
When the trumpet began to sound
The angel rolled the stone away! – stone away!

1
Sister Mary came a-runnin'
At the break of day,
Brought the news from heaven
"The stone is rolled away!"
Well, the angel . . .

2
"I'm a-lookin' for my saviour
Tell me where he lay!
High up on the mountain,
The stone is rolled away!"
Well, the angel . . .

3
"There were soldiers there a-plenty,
Standin' by the door,
But they couldn't hinder
The stone is rolled away!"
Well, the angel . . .

Traditional

Go, Tell It on the Mountain 14

Go, tell it on the mountain,
Over the hills and
everywhere;
Go, tell it on the mountain
That Jesus Christ is born!

1
While shepherds kept their
watching
O'er silent flocks by night,
Behold throughout the
heavens
There shone a holy light:
Go tell it . . .

2
The shepherds feared and
trembled
When lo! above the earth
Rang out the angel chorus
That hailed our Saviour's
birth:
Go tell it . . .

3
Down in a lowly manger
The humble Christ was born,
And God sent us salvation
That blessed Christmas morn:
Go tell it . . .

Traditional

15 Calypso Carol

1
See Him a-lying on a
bed of straw;
A draughty stable with an
open door,
Mary cradling the babe
she bore;
The Prince of Glory is
His name.
O now carry me to
Bethlehem
To see the Lord appear to
men:
Just as poor as was the
stable then,
The Prince of Glory when
He came.

2
Star of silver sweep across
the skies,
Show where Jesus in the
manger lies.
Shepherds swiftly from your
stupor rise
To see the Saviour of the
world.
O now carry me . . .

3
Angels, sing again the song
you sang,
Bring God's glory to the
heart of man:
Sing that Bethlehem's little
baby can
Be Salvation to the soul.
O now carry me . . .

4
Mine are riches—from thy
poverty:
From thine innocence,
eternity;
Mine, forgiveness by thy
death for me,
Child of sorrow for my joy.
O now carry me . . .

M. A. Perry

The Virgin Mary Had a Baby Boy

1

The Virgin Mary had a baby boy,
The Virgin Mary had a baby boy,
The Virgin Mary had a baby boy,
And they say that his name was Jesus.
He come from the glory—
He come from the glorious kingdom;
He come from the glory—
He come from the glorious kingdom;
Oh yes! believer
Oh, yes! believer
He come from the glory—
He come from the glorious kingdom.

2

The angels sang when the baby was born,
The angels sang when the baby was born,
The angels sang when the baby was born,
And proclaimed Him the saviour Jesus.
He come from the glory . . .

3

The wise men saw where the baby was born,
The wise men saw where the baby was born,
The wise men saw where the baby was born,
And they saw that his name was Jesus.
He come from the glory . . .

17 Wise Men, Seeking Jesus

1
Wise men, seeking Jesus,
Travelled from afar,
Guided on their journey
By a beauteous star.

2
But if we desire Him,
He is close at hand;
For our native country
Is our Holy Land.

3
Prayerful souls may find Him
By our quiet lakes,
Meet Him on our hillsides
When the morning breaks.

4
In our fertile cornfields
While the sheaves are bound,
In our busy markets,
Jesus may be found.

5
Fishermen talk with Him
By the great North Sea,
As the first disciples
Did in Galilee.

6
Every peaceful village
In our land might be
Made by Jesus' presence
Like sweet Bethany.

7
He is more than near us,
If we love Him well,
For He seeketh ever
In our hearts to dwell.

James East

Carol of the Birds

1
Whence comes this rush of
wings afar?
Following straight the Noel
star?
Birds from the woods in
wondrous flight,
Bethlehem seek this holy
night.

2
"Tell us, ye birds, why come
ye here,
Into this stable poor and
drear?"
"Hastening we seek the
new-born King,
And all our sweetest music
bring."

3
Hark! how the greenfinch
bears his part,
Nightingale, too, with tender
heart,
Chants from her leafy dark
retreat,
"Re, mi, fa, sol," in accents
sweet.

4
Angels and shepherds, birds
of the sky,
Come where the Son of God
doth lie;
Christ on earth with man
doth dwell,
Join in the shout, "Noel,
Noel!"

Traditional

19 Look for Signs that Summer's Done

1

Look for signs that summer's done,
Winter's drawing near.
Watch the changing colours come,
Turning of the year.
See the flowers' final blaze
In the morning's misty haze,
Sing a thankful song of praise,
Autumn time is here.

2

See the fields are bare and brown,
Feel the nights turn cold.
Lamps are early lit in town,
Hunter's moon shines gold.
Thank you, God, for rest and food,
For the Harvest safely stored,
Sing a song to praise the Lord
As the year grows old.

Peggy Blakeley

20 The Sower

Traditional melody arranged by E. M. Stephenson

1

The sower went out and spread the seed all around,
The sower went out and spread the seed all around,
The sower he spread that seed all around,
He spread that seed all over the ground;
The sower went out and spread the seed all around.

2

Now some of that seed fell down upon the way,
Some of that seed fell down upon the way.
Some of that seed fell upon the way
And the birds came along and took it away;
Now some of that seed fell down upon the way.

3
He watched that seed fall
down on rocky ground,
He watched that seed fall
down on rocky ground,
He watched it fall on rocky
ground,
It grew up quickly, but it
soon fell down;
He watched that seed fall
down on rocky ground.

4
He watched it fall among
some thistle weed,
He watched it fall among
some thistle weed,
It fell among some thistle
weed
And grew, but the thistle
choked that seed.
He watched it fall among
some thistle weed.

But some of that seed fell
down upon good ground.
Some of that seed fell down
upon good ground,
Some of that seed fell upon
good ground,
With lots of fruit it did
abound,
For some of that seed fell
down upon good ground.

6
Now you can listen to the
Word of God,
You can listen to the Word
of God,
But if you listened all you
could
But bore no fruit it would do
no good
For you must act upon the
Word of God.

R. Hawkins

Serving others

21 One Man's Hands

1
One man's hands can't break a prison down,
Two men's hands can't break a prison down,
But if two and two and fifty make a million,
We'll see that day come round,
We'll see that day come round.

2
One man's voice can't shout to make them hear,
Two men's voices can't shout to make them hear,
But if two and two and fifty make a million,
We'll see that day come round,
We'll see that day come round.

3
One man's strength can't ban the atom bomb . . .

4
One man's strength can't break the colour bar . . .

5
One man's eyes can't see the way ahead . . .

Alex Comfort

Reach Out

1
Reach out to your neighbour,
Let him know you really care,
Reach out when he's lonely,
Let him know somebody's
there,
Reach out in his darkness,
When the clouds obscure his
view.
Just walk with him, and talk
with him,
he's waiting there for you.
*Reach out in a world filled
with hopelessness and
pain;*
*Reach out with a hand full of
love!*
*Reach out, the world is
waiting for someone to
lead the way!*
*Reach out, reach out to find
a brand new day!*

2
Reach out to a stranger,
To a man who's lost his way;
Like a sheep without a
shepherd
Who can't find the light of
day;
Reach out, your brother
needs you,
Needs to know he's not
alone!
So tell him of God's mighty
love,
And share with him your
own.
Reach out . . .

3
Reach out, like your saviour,
When he gave his life for
you,
Reach out to all the people
Who don't know what to do;
Reach out and tell of Jesus,
Who has done His greatest
part;
Just share the love I'm
singing of;
Reach out with all your
heart!
Reach out . . .

Roger Copeland

23 The Good Samaritan

1
There was a man on a long,
long journey-o,
On the road from Jerusalem
to Jericho.
The way was stony and
all-aloney-o
With many a twist and wind.

2
And thieves were lurking
round the rocks and lying
low,
On the road from Jerusalem
to Jericho.
They robbed him and beat
him till his blood did flow,
And left him half dead
behind.

3
Came a priest from the great
big temple-o,
On the road from Jerusalem
to Jericho.
Did he stop to help him?
Oh dear no;
He just left him lying there.

4
Came a Levite, a very clever
fellow,
On the road from Jerusalem
to Jericho
He saw him and walked past
and on did go
With his nose in the air.

5
Then a Samaritan with his
little donkey-o,
On the road from Jerusalem
to Jericho
Bandaged him and brought
him to an inn-o,
And paid for him to stay.

6
All our life is along, long
journey-o,
On the road from Jerusalem
to Jericho.
We should help everyone
that we meet, and so
Why don't we start today.

Mother Mary Oswin

Tell Me

1
Tell me, why are there people around me
Hungry and needy, and lonely and sad?
The world must be mad.
Why can't we give
So that others may live?

2
Tell me, why is there hate between races?
What does it matter, the colour or creed,
When your brother's in need,
When will man conquer his greed?

3
Tell me, why are men fighting
And why is war so inviting?
Yet men delight in,
Killing each other, I'd love to discover why.

4
Tell me, Something that I could do,
Something that would be positive,
Useful and kind,
Oh help me to find,
Some way to serve mankind.

Colin Williams

25 The Bird's Song

1
I perched in the branches and heard what He said,
The God of creation providing our bread,
The loaves that He blessed were enough for them all,
Including twelve baskets for us, I recall.
For all men are brothers, if each one would share
Then none need go hungry and live in despair,
But some grasp for two loaves, while some have a crust,
And some cannot even find crumbs in the dust.

2
I perched on a branch of the sycamore tree
Where Jesus knew Zacchaeus wanted to see;
And God's like a father who hears every sound,
And knows even sparrows that fall to the ground.
For all men . . .

3
I perched in the branches and heard what He said:
'The birds have their nesting place—I have no bed.
The truth that I speak is like seed, and I pray
The fowls of the air will not take it away.'
For all men . . .

Cecily Taylor

Only Jesus

26

1
Who took fish and bread?
Hungry people fed?
Who changed water into
wine?
Who made well the sick,
who made see the blind?
Who touched earth with feet
divine?
Only Jesus, Only Jesus,
Only He has done this:
Who made live the dead?
Truth and kindness spread?
Only Jesus did all this.

2
Who walked dusty road?
Cared for young and old?
Who sat children on His
knee?
Who spoke words so wise?
Filled men with surprise,
Who gave all, but charged
no fee?
Only Jesus, Only Jesus,
Only He has done this:
Who in death and grief spoke
peace to a thief?
Only Jesus did all this.

3
Who soared through the air?
Joined His Father there?
He has you and me in view:
He, who this has done, is
God's only Son,
And he's int'rested in you.
Only Jesus, Only Jesus,
Only He has done this:
He can change a heart, give a
new fresh start,
Only He can do this.

Betty Lou Mills

27 Allelu!

Allelu! Allelu! Ev'rybody
sing Allelu!
For the Lord has risen,
it is true –
Ev'rybody sing Allelu!

1
God said He would send His
Son, Allelu, Allelu!
And salvation would be won,
Alleluia!
Allelu! . . .

2
Christ was born in
Bethlehem, Allelu, Allelu!
So that man would live
again, Alleluia!
Allelu! . . .

3
Thirty years He walked the
land, Allelu, Allelu!
To all in need He lent His
hand, Alleluia!
Allelu! . . .

4
On the hard wood of the
cross, Allelu, Allelu!
He suffered and He died for
us, Alleluia!
Allelu! . . .

5
On the third day He did rise,
Allelu, Allelu!
Now He lives no more to die,
Alleluia!
Allelu! . . .

6
Now we too can live anew,
Allelu, Allelu!
Live in Him need all we do,
Alleluia!
Allelu! . . .

Ray Repp

O when the Saints go Marching in

1
O when the saints go
marching in,
O when the saints go
marching in;
O Lord I want to be among
the number
When the saints go
marching in.

2
O when they crown Him
Lord of all,
O when they crown Him
Lord of all;
O Lord, I want to be among
the number
When they crown Him
Lord of all.

3
O when all knees bow at
His name,
O when all knees bow at
His name;
O Lord, I want to be among
the number
When all knees bow at
His name.

4
O when they sing the
Saviour's praise,
O when they sing the
Saviour's praise;
O Lord, I want to be among
the number
When they sing the Saviour's
praise.

5
O when the saints go
marching in,
O when the saints go
marching in;
O Lord, I want to be among
the number
When the saints go
marching in.

Traditional

29 Sing Life, Sing Love, Sing Jesus

Sing life, sing love, sing
Jesus,
Sing out wherever you are.
Sing life, sing love, sing
Jesus,
Sing out wherever you are.

1
Life is a thing we can use or
abuse,
Life can be great or a bore.
It all depends on the way
that we choose,
Whether we notice or just
ignore God's love.
Sing life . . .

2
Love is a thing we can give or
can take,
Love can bring life or bring
death.
I can love myself and be on
the make
Or live for others, till my last
breath like Jesus.
Sing life . . .

3
Jesus gives life, in love he
died,
Jesus the truth and the way.
Although he is betrayed and
denied,
In men his life and love live
on today.
Sing life . . .

Pete Lewis

Come and Praise

Start with Chorus:

Come and praise the Lord
our King, Hallelujah,
Come and praise the Lord
our King, Hallelujah.

1
Christ was born in Bethlehem,
Hallelujah,
Son of God and Son of Man,
Hallelujah:
Come and praise . . .

2
He grew up an earthly child,
Hallelujah,
Of the world, but undefiled,
Hallelujah:
Come and praise . . .

3
Jesus died at Calvary,
Hallelujah,
Rose again triumphantly,
Hallelujah:
Come and praise . . .

4
He will cleanse us from our
sin, Hallelujah,
If we live by faith in Him,
Hallelujah:
Come and praise . . .

5
We will live with Him one
day, Hallelujah,
And for ever with Him stay,
Hallelujah:
Come and praise . . .

Traditional

31 Here's Joy

1
Bursting into life
With an earthquake's force,
Just like fireworks tossed
Comes joy!

2
Beat it on the drum,
Like the thunder's roar,
Let the storm outpour
Our joy!

3
Swing the clarinet
Into sparkling song,
And we'll march along
With joy!

4
Blow it on the sax
With a brilliant flair,
Music fills the air
With joy!

5
Plucking the guitar
To a throbbing beat,
We will tap the feet
With joy!

6
As the organ chords
Add their melody,
We'll make our choice
In joy!

7
And the Son of Man
Gives to all their lead,
It's just what we need
For joy!

8
So we join as one
Giving Him the praise
For these glad new days
Of joy!

9
Let the whole world swing
And the cosmos ring,
As we celebrate
Our joy!

Valerie M. Dunn

He Keeps Me Singing a Happy Song 32

He keeps me singing a happy
song,
He keeps me singing it all
day long;
Although the days may be
drear,
He always is near
And that's why me heart is
always filled with song:
I'm singing, singing, all day
long!
He keeps me all day long!

Howard Stevenson

33 Praise the Lord, Ye Heavens Adore Him

1
Praise the Lord! Ye Heavens, adore Him;
Praise Him, angels in the height;
Sun and moon, rejoice before Him;
Praise Him, all ye stars and light.

2
Praise the Lord, for He hath spoken;
Worlds His mighty voice obeyed;
Laws, that never shall be broken,
For their guidance He hath made.

3
Praise the Lord, for He is glorious;
Never shall His promise fail;
God hath made His saints victorious;
Sin and death shall not prevail.

4
Praise the God of our salvation;
Hosts on high His power proclaim;
Heaven and earth, and all creation,
Laud and magnify His name.

Anon

Fisherman Peter

1
Fisherman Peter, on the sea,
Drop your net, boy, and
follow me!
Fisherman Peter, on the sea,
Drop your net, boy, and
follow me!

2
Rich young ruler, plain to
see,
Can't love money and follow
me!
Rich young ruler, plain to
see,
Can't love money and follow
me!

3
Lonely Zaccheus in the tree,
Love your neighbour and
follow me!
Lonely Zaccheus in the tree,
Love your neighbour and
follow me!

4
Nicodemus Pharisee,
New life comes when you
follow me!
Nicodemus Pharisee,
New life comes when you
follow me!

5
Doubting Thomas, from
doubt be free,
Stop your doubting and
follow me!
Doubting Thomas, from
doubt be free,
Stop your doubting and
follow me!

Traditional

35 Peter's Song

1
He lived for me, to show me
what my life could be,
He lived for me, so that I'd
have the vision to see
That we live at our best
when we give to others
And selfishness is defied,
He lived for me, a challenge,
a friend and a guide.

2
He died for me, I was there
in the crowd at the end,
He died for me, I denied him
though he was my friend.
His death on the cross was a
futile end
To a life that had hardly
begun,
He died for me, and forgave
me for what I had done.

3
He lives in me, when I follow
the steps he would take,
He lives in me, when I help
anyone for his sake,
His hands are mine and his
power's in me
When I take the way he
would go,
He lives in me—that's the
greatest joy I know.

Stephen Knott

What a Friend

1
What a friend we have in
  Jesus,
All our sins and grief to bear!
What a privilege to carry
Everything to God in prayer.
O what peace we often
  forfeit,
O what needless pain we
  bear
All because we do not carry
Everything to God in prayer.

2
Have we trials and
  temptations?
Is there trouble anywhere?
We should never be
  discouraged:
Take it to the Lord in prayer.
Can we find a friend so
  faithful,
Who will all our sorrows
  share?
Jesus knows our every
  weakness:
Take it to the Lord in prayer.

3
Are we weak and heavy-
  laden,
Cumbered with a load of
  care?
Jesus only is our refuge:
Take it to the Lord in prayer.
Do thy friends despise,
  forsake thee?
Take it to the Lord in prayer;
In His arms He'll take and
  shield thee!
Thou wilt find a solace there.

4
What a friend we have in
  Jesus,
All our sins and grief to bear!
What a privilege to carry
Everything to God in prayer.
O what peace we often
  forfeit,
O what needless pain we
  bear
All because we do not carry
Everything to God in prayer.

J. M. Scriven

37 Can It be True?

1
Can it be true, the things
 they say of You?
You walked this earth
 sharing with friends You
 knew
All that they had the work,
 the joy, the pain,
That we might find the way
 to heav'n again.

2
And day by day You still
 return this way;
But we recall there was a
 debt to pay:
Out of Your love for Your
 own world above,
You left that holy thing,
 Your endless love to prove.

3
Can it be true, the things
 they did to You—
The death, the shame, and
 were Your friends so few?
Yet You returned again alive
 and free—
Can it be true, my Lord, it
 had to be.

Brother William

Follow my Leader

1
The journey of life may be easy, may be hard,
There'll be dangers on the way;
With Christ at my side I'll do battle as I ride
'Gainst the foe that would lead me astray.
Will you ride, ride, ride with the King of Kings,
Will you follow my leader true;
Will you shout Hosanna to the lowly Son of God,
Who died for me and you.

2
My burden is light and a song is in my heart,
As I travel on life's way;
For Christ is my Lord and He's given me His word,
That by my side He'll stay.
Will you ride . . .

3
When doubts arise and when tears are in my eyes,
When all seems lost to me;
With Christ as my Guide I can smile what e'er betide,
For He my strength will be.
Will you ride . . .

4
I'll follow my Leader where ever He may go,
For Jesus is my Friend;
He'll lead me on to the place where He has gone,
When I come to my journey's end.
Will you ride . . .

Valerie Collison

39 At the Name of Jesus

1
At the name of Jesus
Every knee shall bow,
Every tongue confess Him
King of glory now;
'Tis the Father's pleasure
We should call Him Lord,
Who from the beginning
Was the mighty Word.

2
At His voice creation
Sprang at once to sight,
All the angel faces,
All the hosts of light;
Thrones and dominations,
Stars upon their way,
All the heavenly orders
In their great array.

3
Humbled for a season
To receive a name
From the lips of sinners,
Unto whom He came;
Faithfully He bore it
Spotless to the last;
Brought it back victorious
When from death He passed.

4
Name Him, brothers, name
Him
With love strong as death,
But with awe and wonder,
And with bated breath;
He is God the Saviour,
He is Christ the Lord,
Ever to be worshipped,
Trusted and adored.

5
In your hearts enthrone Him;
There let him subdue
All that is not holy,
All that is not true;
Crown Him as your Captain
In temptation's hour,
Let His will enfold you
In its light and power.

6
Brothers, this Lord Jesus
Shall return again,
With His Father's glory,
With His angel train;
For all wreaths of empire
Meet upon His brow,
And our hearts confess Him
King of glory now.

C. M. Noel

O Jesus I Have Promised

40

1
O Jesus, I have promised
To serve Thee to the end;
Be Thou for ever near me,
My Master and my Friend;
I shall not fear the battle
If Thou art by my side,
Nor wander from the pathway
If Thou wilt be my Guide.

2
O let me feel Thee near me,
The world is ever near;
I see the sights that dazzle,
The tempting sounds I hear;
My foes are ever near me,
Around me and within;
But Jesus, draw Thou nearer,
And shield my soul from sin.

3
O let me hear Thee speaking
In accents clear and still,
Above the storms of passion,
The murmurs of self-will;
O speak to reassure me,
To hasten, or control;
O speak, and make me listen,
Thou Guardian of my soul.

4
O Jesus, Thou hast promised
To all who follow Thee,
That where Thou art in glory,
There shall Thy servants be;
And, Jesus, I have promised
To serve Thee to the end:
O give me grace to follow,
My Master and my Friend.

5
O let me see Thy footmarks,
And in them plant mine own;
My hope to follow duly
Is in Thy strength alone.
O guide me, call me, draw me,
Uphold me to the end;
And then in heaven receive me,
My Saviour and my Friend.

J. E. Bode

41 We are climbing Jacob's ladder

1
We are climbing Jacob's ladder
We are climbing Jacob's ladder
We are climbing Jacob's ladder
Soldiers of the cross.

2
Ev'ry rung goes higher 'n' higher
Ev'ry rung goes higher 'n' higher
Ev'ry rung goes higher 'n' higher
Soldiers of the Cross.

3
Sinner do you love my Jesus?
Sinner do you love my Jesus?
Sinner do you love my Jesus?
Soldiers of the Cross.

4
If you love Him, why not serve Him?
If you love Him, why not serve Him?
If you love Him, why not serve Him?
Soldiers of the Cross.

5
Faithful prayer will make a soldier
Faithful prayer will make a soldier
Faithful prayer will make a soldier
Soldiers of the Cross

6
We are climbing higher 'n' higher
We are climbing higher 'n' higher
We are climbing higher 'n' higher
Soldiers of the Cross.

Traditional

Hands of Jesus

1

Hands of Jesus, take the
bread,
As long ago
While here below;
Take the bread at morning
time.

2

Hands of Jesus, bless the
bread;
Bless it to me,
That it may be
Living bread at morning time.

3

Hands of Jesus, break the
bread,
And break it small,
And grant to all
Broken bread at morning
time.

4

Hands of Jesus, give the
bread,
That with Thy Word,
We may be fed;
Hear our prayer at morning
time.

G. Brattle

43 Kum ba yah (Be with Us)

1
Kum ba yah, my Lord,
Kum ba yah!
Kum ba yah, my Lord,
Kum ba yah!
Kum ba yah, my Lord,
Kum ba yah!
O Lord, Kum ba yah.

2
Someone's crying, Lord,
Kum ba yah . . .

3
Someone's singing, Lord,
Kum ba yah . . .

4
Someone's praying, Lord,
Kum ba yah . . .

West Indian Traditional

Thank You

1
Thank you for waking me this morning;
Thank you for this and ev'ry day,
Thank you that my cares and worries
you can take away.

2
Thank you for my friends and brothers;
Thank you for all the men that live,
Thank you that even greatest enemies
I can forgive.

3
Thank you for my work and leisure;
Thank you for every pleasure small,
Thank you for music, light and gladness,
Thank you for them all.

4
Thank you for my food and lodgings;
Thank you for my life and health,
Thank you that our work and schooling
can produce such wealth.

5
Thank you for your word and guidance;
Thank you for your presence here,
Thank you that you love all people
those both far and near.

6
Thank you Lord, for speaking to us;
Thank you for the way you care,
Thank you that you come among us
In our lives to share.

7
Thank you that your love is endless;
Thank you that your word is true,
Thank you that you make me feel
so thankful, as I do.

Pete Lewis

45 The Lord's Prayer

Our Father who art in
Heaven,
Hallowed be Thy Name.
Thy Kingdom come, Thy will
be done,
Hallowed be Thy Name.
On the earth as it is in
Heaven,
Hallowed be Thy Name.
Give us this day our daily
bread,
Hallowed be Thy Name.
Forgive us all our trespasses,
Hallowed be Thy Name.
As we forgive those who
trespass against us,
Hallowed be Thy Name.
And lead us not into
temptation,
Hallowed be Thy Name.
But deliver us from all that is
evil,
Hallowed be Thy Name.
For Thine is the Kingdom,
the Power and the Glory,
Hallowed be Thy Name.
For ever and for ever and
ever,
Hallowed be Thy Name.
Amen, Amen, it shall be so,
Hallowed be Thy Name.
Amen, Amen, it shall be so,
Hallowed be Thy Name.

West Indian Traditional

The Lord's My Shepherd

1
The Lord's my shepherd, I'll not want
He makes me down to lie
In pastures green; He leadeth me
The quiet waters by.

2
My soul He doth restore again,
And me to walk doth make
Within the paths of righteousness,
E'en for His own name's sake.

3
Yea, though I walk in death's dark vale,
Yet will I fear no ill;
For thou art with me, and Thy rod
And staff me comfort still.

4
My table Thou hast furnished
In presence of my foes;
My head Thou dost with oil anoint
And my cup over flows.

5
Goodness and mercy all my life
Shall surely follow me,
And in God's house for evermore
My dwelling-place shall be.

Psalm 23
Scottish Psalter

47 Amazing Grace

1
Amazing grace—how sweet
the sound—
That saved a wretch like me!
I once was lost but now am
found,
Was blind but now I see.

2
'Twas grace that taught my
heart to fear,
And grace my fears relieved;
How precious did that grace
appear
The hour I first believed!

3
Through many dangers, toils
and snares
I have already come;
'Tis grace hath brought me
safe thus far,
And grace will lead me home.

4
When we've been there ten
thousand years,
Bright shining as the sun,
We've no less days to sing
God's praise
Than when we'd first begun.

John Newton

Hundreds and Thousands

48

1
There are hundreds of sparrows, thousands, millions,
They're two a penny, far too many there must be;
There are hundreds and thousands, millions of sparrows,
But God knows ev'ry-one and God knows me.

2
There are hundreds of flowers, thousands, millions,
And flowers fair the meadows wear for all to see;
There are hundreds and thousands, millions of flowers,
But God knows ev'ry-one and God knows me.

3
There are hundreds of planets, thousands, millions,
Way out in space each has a place by God's decree;
There are hundreds and thousands, millions of planets,
But God knows ev'ry-one and God knows me.

4
There are hundreds of children, thousands, millions,
And yet their names are written on God's memory,
There are hundreds and thousands, millions of children,
But God knows ev'ry-one and God knows me!
But God knows ev'ry-one and God knows me.

J. Gowans

49 They Say He's Wonderful

1
He makes the rain to fall,
He sees the wheat grow tall,
The root, the shoot and soon the fruit,
The root, the shoot and soon the fruit,
It shows He cares for all.
They say He's wonderful,
They say He's wonderful,
The sun, the moon, the stars that shine,
The sun, the moon, the stars that shine
Say God is wonderful.

2
When I see babies small,
And I hear children call,
And think of family life and fun,
And think of family life and fun,
I know He's behind it all.
They say . . .

3
The love men have for Him,
Such love death cannot dim,
Of small and great of rich and poor,
Of small and great of rich and poor,
Love like this comes from Him.
They say . . .

4
And I know He's wonderful,
I know He's wonderful,
The Son of God who died for me,
The Son of God who died for me,
I know He's wonderful.
They say . . .

Hugh Pollock

He's Got the Whole World in His Hands

1

He's got the whole world in
his hands,
He's got the whole world in
his hands,
He's got the whole world in
his hands,
He's got the whole world in
his hands.

2

He's got you and me brother,
in his hands,
He's got you and me brother,
in his hands,
He's got you and me brother,
in his hands,
He's got the whole world in
his hands.

3

He's got you and me sister,
in his hands,
He's got you and me sister,
in his hands,
He's got you and me sister,
in his hands,
He's got the whole world in
his hands.

4

He's got everybody in his
hands,
He's got everybody in his
hands,
He's got everybody in his
hands,
He's got the whole world in
his hands.

Traditional

51 God Bless the Grass

1
God bless the grass that
grows through the crack,
They roll the concrete over
it to try and keep it back.
The concrete gets tired of
what it has to do,
It breaks and it buckles and
the grass grows through;
And God bless the grass.

2
God bless the truth that
fights toward the sun,
They roll the lies over it and
hope that it is done.
It moves through the ground
and reaches for the air,
And after a while it is
growing everywhere;
And God bless the truth.

3
God bless the grass that
breaks through cement.
It's green and it's tender
and it's easily bent,
But after a while it lifts
up its head,
For the grass is living and
the stone is dead;
And God bless the grass.

4
God bless the grass that's
gentle and low,
Its roots they are deep and
its will is to grow.
And God bless the truth,
the friend of the poor,
And the wild grass growing
at the poor man's door;
And God bless the grass.

Malvina Reynolds

52

Spirit of God

Sister Miriam Therese Winter

1

Spirit of God in the clear running water,
Blowing to greatness the trees on the hill—
Spirit of God in the finger of morning,
Fill the earth, bring it to birth,
And blow where you will.
Blow, blow, blow till I be
But breath of the Spirit blowing in me.

2

Down in the meadow the willows are moaning,
Sheep in the pastureland cannot lie still;
Spirit of God, creation is groaning—
Fill the earth, bring it to birth,
And blow where you will.
Blow, blow . . .

3

I saw the scar of a year that lay dying,
heard the lament of a lone whip-poor-will;
Spirit of God, see that cloud crying—
Fill the earth, bring it to birth,
And blow where you will.
Blow, blow . . .

4

Spirit of God, ev'ry man's heart is lonely,
Watching and waiting and hungry until—
Spirit of God, man longs that you only
Fulfill the earth, bring it to birth,
And blow where you will.
Blow, blow . . .

Sister Miriam Therese Winter

53 The Gift of Water

1
Water in the snow:
the mountains sparkle white;
the muffled trees bow low,
burdened with light.

2
Water in the rain:
the wheat is growing tall;
the fields are packed with
  grain—
plenty for all.

3
Water in the ground;
where earth is cracked and
  dry
down deep the well has
  found
ample supply.

4
Water from the stream:
the tap runs fresh and clear
the clothes, now washed
  and clean
blow in the air.

5
Water fills the dam:
it tumbles from the height
and falling, gives to man
power and light.

6
Water in the sea:
the trawling nets unfurl;
the oyster in the deep
treasures in pearl.

7
Water gives us life
and beauty, power and
  food—
praise God, who in his love
made all things good.

Brian A. Wren
(1936–)

Teach Me How to Look Lord

1
When the world is dark and dreary
There is beauty still around;
Hiding in so many places
Waiting to be found.
Teach me how to look, Lord,
Teach me how to see.
All the wondrous treasures
In this world for me.

2
Many faces, hard and stony
Hide the jewel of a smile;
It is there to be discovered
Waiting all the while.
Teach me how to look, Lord,
How to preserve
For the friendly spirit
That can be so near.

3
When a heart is like a desert,
Kindness hides among the weeds;
It is there just for the finding,
Love is all it needs.
Teach me how to look, Lord,
Open wide my eyes
So that I can find, Lord,
Goodness in disguise.

4
If we look both long and deeply
Into one another's hearts,
We will find the understanding
Tolerance imparts.
Teach me how to look, Lord,
Let me not be blind
To the strength of others
There for me to find.

Peter Dacre

55 The Gospel Train

1

The gospel train's a-coming,
I hear it close at hand
I hear those car wheels
rumbling and moving
through the land:
Get on board, little children,
get on board,
Little children, get on
board, little children,
There's room for many'a
more

2

I hear the bell and whistle,
a coming round the curve,
She's playing all the steam
and power, and straining
every nerve:
Get on board . . .

3

The fare is cheap and all
can go, the rich and poor
are there,
No second class aboard that
train, no difference in the
fare:
Get on board . . .

4

No signal for another train to
follow on the line,
O sinner, you're for ever lost
if once you're left behind:
Get on board . . .

5

She's nearing now the
station—O sinner, don't be
vain;
O come and get your ticket,
and be ready for that train:
Get on board . . .

Traditional

Joy of living
The Star Song

Girls and boys many as the stars,
Each and every one, loved as a son
By this God of ours.
Who can count the children of the earth?
Each and every one loved as a son
From his day of birth.

Who can count the stars that fly across the sky at night
Who can tell how wonderful is that shimmering sight?
If they are made of stone and fire and God holds them above
Then we who are his children will we not have his love?

Girls and boys many as the stars . . .

Malcolm Stewart

57 I Know Where I'm Going

1
I know where I'm going
And I know who's going with
me.
I know why there's music
In the quiet summer morning.
I found a wealth of gold,
And silver I have plenty;
I found a light to guide me
When my way gets dark and
stormy.

2
Where are you going,
Who will walk beside you?
When the night is gloomy,
Where is the light to guide
you?
And where's your gold
And your silver brightly
shining?
Who writes the music
In the quiet summer morning?

3
I'm going where He goes,
And He'll be there beside me,
The love for which He died,
Is all I need to guide me.
And He's my gold
And my silver brightly
shining!
He writes the music
In the quiet summer morning.

I know where I'm going,
But where are you going?

Scottish Folk Song

Haul Away

Haul, haul away.
Haul, haul away.
Cast the nets wide and sink the nets deep.
And it's haul, haul away.

1
Oh, he sat in the boat and he spoke to the crowd.
Haul, haul away.
And his voice wasn't soft and his voice wasn't loud.
Haul, haul away.
And he spoke of the just and the pure and the free,
and his voice caught the air like a net in the sea.
And it's haul . . .

2
He said: "Cast your nets wide where the water is deep".
Haul, haul away.
"Oh, cast the nets wide and sink the nets deep."
Haul, haul away.
"Though we've worked through the night and we've nothing to show,
we will try once again just because you say so."
And it's haul . . .

3
Oh the catch it was huge and the boat it was small.
Haul, haul away.
His friends came to help when they heard Peter call.
Haul, haul away.
"You must leave us," said Peter, "for we're men of sin."
But he said: "Come with me and be fishers of men."
And it's haul . . .

Michael Cockett

59 Sing Hosanna

1
Give me joy in my heart,
keep me praising,
Give me joy in my heart, I
pray;
Give me joy in my heart,
keep me praising,
Keep me praising till the
break of day:
Sing Hosanna! Sing Hosanna!
Sing Hosanna to the King of
Kings!
Sing Hosanna! Sing Hosanna!
Sing Hosanna to the King.

2
Give me peace in my heart,
keep me loving,
Give me peace in my heart, I
pray,
Give me peace in my heart,
keep me loving,
Keep me loving till the break
of day:
Sing Hosanna! . . .

3
Give me love in my heart,
keep me serving,
Give me love in my heart, I
pray,
Give me love in my heart,
keep me serving,
Keep me serving till the
break of day.
Sing Hosanna! . . .

Traditional

Joy Is Like the Rain

1
I saw rain-drops on my window,
Joy is like the rain.
Laughter runs across my pain,
Slips away and comes again.
Joy is like the rain.

2
I saw clouds upon a mountain,
Joy is like a cloud.
Sometimes silver, sometimes grey,
Always sun not far away.
Joy is like a cloud.

3
I saw Christ in wind and thunder,
Joy is tried by storm.
Christ asleep within my boat,
Whipped by wind, yet still afloat.
Joy is tried by storm.

4
I saw rain-drops on the river,
Joy is like the rain,
Bit by bit the river grows,
Till all at once it overflows.
Joy is like the rain.

Sister Miriam Therese Winter